The Responses of My Soul

Poetry With A Purpose
Having My Way With Words

S. LENNARD SMITH

Published By:
Spencer Publishing
Los Angeles, California 90016
Smith-spencer@hotmail.com

Cover design: Jay De Vance, III
First printing: January 2013
Library of Congress Control Number: 2012924202
ISBN: 978-0-615-74686-9
10987654321

ACKNOWLEDGMENTS

First, I would like to thank some people with whom I have shared life experiences. I would like to thank God; my parents, Irene and Robert; my wife, Karen; my children, Spencer, Makita, and Sabre; my siblings, Floyd, Lloyd, Minda, Millicent, William and Melody; my in-laws, Arthur and Hattie; and a host of friends and family.

May God continue to bless you all.

$\mathcal{I}$ would also like to pay homage to the Poet William "Smokey" Robinson and to my first black president of the United States, President Barack Obama.

$\mathcal{F}$or your reading pleasure, I thought I would share the **Responses of My Soul**—from love to politics throughout my life, so far.

Oh Lord, please give me the strength to endure what I must in order to achieve what I need to succeed.

— MY PRAYER

You won't survive on the dance floor of life if you don't have a good drummer.

So, take care of your heart, because it beats for life. Keep the rhythm and stay in time.

TABLE OF CONTENTS

Love is You

Love is you, I know this to be true; it seems you do all you can to help me from feeling blue. I see no way in this world to repay you.

But this I do know; I would like to spend the rest of my life making passionate payments to you.

With the affection and contentment you convey, knowing that you are beside me; neither pain nor sorrow is tolerable.

The prayers I've asked from up above, you entered my life and I knew that you were love.

Sweet Love

I know I'm blessed from up above, because I'm showered with her sweet love.

She makes love to me that's so sweet, it causes me to weep. She has the kind of love that's so sweet, you can't find it in the clubs, malls or streets; her sweet love is so strong it's homegrown.

Her kindness flows through her veins, to give sweet love is no strain. Her loving way removes all pain.

When she gives me her love that's so sweet, it keeps me begging for a repeat.

I know I'm blessed from up above, because I'm showered with her sweet love.

Love Expression

Just as sure as I can count on the sun to set in the west, I know I can always count on you to give me your best.

And I would like to take this time to tell you how much you stay on my mind, and how hard it is for me to keep track of time. Throughout my days, my head is in a haze.

I adore the love we share to its very core. And every day I want you more and more. You are the reason I breathe; I think of you between every time I inhale and exhale.

Therefore, I am compelled to profess the blissful affection your touch has cast upon my life. Your love feels so right.

I will hold on with all my might, I will not let go to save my life.

A profound tender you have placed in my heart, no one can ever tear us apart.

The ecstasy and pleasantries you provide to me makes me see that you are the only one for me.

Your love fills me up abundantly and this profuse affection is my—love expression.

❦

D.O.C.

Above all things on Earth, your love has inspired me in every way.

When I wake up to start my day on bended knees, a prayer for you I'll say.

Your touch motivates my every move. The words you speak aim to soothe.

I pour out my gratitude on to you. If you were not here, I wouldn't know what to do.

When I need you, you never hesitate. After a long and stressful day, I love the way your kisses revive me.

When I look in your eyes, I see no disguise. I think, I must testify, my love for you I will not hide. Your lovely smile brightens my darkest days. It helps me find a better way.

You're my addiction. I am like an addict that can't kick the habit.

If someone would offer me help, I could not follow the twelve steps. You are my drug of choice. I'd shake and shiver if I couldn't hear your voice. I'm energized.

You've had me mesmerized. I'm glad to have you as my own supply. I will be hooked until the day I die.

My Queen

To love her is to know her; she's as beautiful as the setting of the sun.

When she walks into the room, she sets a tone, letting you know she has a mind of her own.

Her black skin is worth more than gold, and she has so much soul.

I'll do anything to make her my Queen.

And when she enters your space, you can feel her grace. When she steps on the scene, she can make the birds sing.

To say she's pretty is an understatement; her beauty is more than skin deep and personality makes her complete.

She's in a Cleopatra and Nefertiti league; with this lady I'm so intrigued, She's so smart you wouldn't believe.

She's just the kind of lady I would love to meet. Spending my Saturday nights discussing her feelings and rubbing her feet.

I swear, if I ever see her again, I'll offer a ring and ask to be her King.

❦

The Contents of Your Heart

I've been to a lot of places all over the world, and met some of the loveliest ladies, and prettiest girls.

But, your rare quality comes around once in a lifetime. And with the contents of your heart, makes you so hard to find.

Your love grows definitely; you know it promotes my chivalry.

Your angelic ways and affectionate touch are the pure ingredients that make me love you so much.

So many women think they have to use what they've got to get what they want.

And, some of them can forget to use their hearts from the jump.

Your passion is straight from the heart with unconditional love, as if someone has released the doves.

It's a certain quality that sets you apart, with the loving contents of your heart.

❧

Never Imagined

I never imagined feeling like this, as I look back and reminisce.

I thought of a mediocre love affair at first glare turned out to be a love beyond compare.

This girl, to me felt like no other. And when we're together, she would always call me her lover.

The way she touched me was above average; in my dreams I could picture a marriage with a horse and carriage.

I never knew my sunshine would turn to rain, when she yelled out another lover's name.

I was greeted with despair when she needed to clear the air. She told me that her lovers came in pairs. When we met, I didn't know I had to share.

To my dismay, she needed a silent partner of a three-way.

At a crossroad is where I stood; I would erase this lover's memory if I could. But as I sit and reminisce, thinking about her love, I can't resist.

Come Back, Baby

As I look in the mirror and stare into my eyes, I'm wondering what's going on inside. What's this pain that keeps me calling your name.

I bear the shame of playing a game. I was known as a good fellow, full of jolly, but now I've surrender to melancholy.

Come back, baby, come back; this despair I cannot bear.

There will be no more games; my loss is driving me insane. I thought it was cool to play a game without rules, oh what a fool.

I took your love for fun, and I was like a dog on the run, but I've seen Cesar Millan.

Come back, baby, come back; every minute feels like a heart attack. Come back, baby.

I'll pay any cost to get back the loss; my conscious is telling me that it's my fault. What a lesson love has taught, knowing that it can't be bought.

Come back, baby, come back; this despair I cannot bear.

A pretty face can never replace your love in this case; their sexual healing would be just a waste. I missed the way your lips taste. Can't wait to have you face to face.

Come back, baby, come back; I'm sorry and that's a fact.

It's Driving Me Crazy

It was a week ago today when my lady phoned me up to say she needed space or to take a break, in any case. And I asked if I could hold her body for just one more time, and she declined.

I had a stupid look on my face, and in my mouth a bad taste. My heart said, "Keep the faith."

But my stomach wanted to regurgitate, as I hyperventilate.

That's when I knew I had to face my reality. When all I saw was a catastrophe.

My legs said, "Stand strong, and keep it moving." Because my lady I knew I was losing; in my mind I had to agree and break free.

It was Friday night, so my feet said, "Let's hit the nearest hot spot." As I stepped inside, I couldn't believe my eyes; could it be a figure that resembled my lady's anatomy, so I approached from behind.

With the loud music, my mind spoke up once again, and my mouth helped out with a shout.

Ooh yeah, you got a body like my lady's, and it's driving me crazy! You mind taking her place and letting me hold you around your waist!

This girl had a face of a baby, but a body like a lady. I'm telling you it was driving me crazy. So I grabbed her hand, and once again spoke these words.

Ooh yeah, you got a body like my lady's, and it's driving me crazy! You mind taking her place and letting me hold you around your waist!

We danced until the lights came on, and I held her body to every song. My lady will be happy to see that I've found therapy.

Putting Away My Pride

Girl, I used to pride myself on keeping my love inside, and the love for you I would always try to hide.

Then my heart said to me, "You have to put your pride aside, to cultivate the love that is so hard to find."

You see, girl, I need your love, like a seed needs soil.

And just to think of losing your love makes my blood boil.

I can't sleep from worrying about our love meeting a defeat.

Baby I'm putting away my pride to cultivate this love I have inside.

With friends, I seem so secure, appearing to be the man. But with you and me torn. I'll be worst than a woman scorned.

Baby I'm putting away my pride to cultivate this love I have inside.

A sacrifice I'm willing to make, and I 'm not gonna hesitate. I'm so hell bent, 'cause I know your love is heaven sent.

Baby I'm putting away my pride this love for you I can't hide.

I'm putting away my pride, and I'm gonna nurture this love, and I cannot lie. I'm putting away my pride.

❧

Love Soldier

Your Highness
My Soldier is at attention, I pledge my allegiance to your passion, and I want to make love to you in every fashion.

Your satisfaction is the tour of duty.

A journey of lovemaking I want to deploy.

My priority is to serve you and explore, even in my afterworld, I'll love you more.

This emotional sensation gives off such a vibration it keep my adrenaline racing.

I'm a true love soldier; soldier of lovemaking.

Under your command, I'll try to kill it, my heart is purple if that's the color of love.

An honorable love soldier is what I enlisted to be, but if dishonorable, then use your sex as a weapon and come from your hips, 'cause I want to be pussy whipped!

I am your true love soldier with skills so erotic I must be patriotic.

I'm proud to be loyal and devoted. For your love I'll travel near and far, 'cause I'd rather make love than war.
I salute and protect your love. I'm your true love soldier.

I'm So Lucky

I've never been the kind of guy that believed in luck, until I found you. The feeling you give me is like some type of magic or voodoo. Luck was like love, a supernatural force I never knew. I had no clue. When I hold your hand, I feel like a lucky man.

I'm so lucky it's clear to see; you release the endorphins in me. No superstition or witchcraft. Just repetitive pleasure is what I got; it keeps me screaming jackpot.

I wanna thank the Lord, 'cause to find a love like yours is hard. I have never had such good fortune. It must be beginner's luck or a mystery. A love like yours should go down in history.

I'm so lucky it's clear to see; you release the endorphins in me. No superstition or witchcraft. Just repetitive pleasure is what I got; it keeps me screaming jackpot.

Rabbit's foot, four-leaf clovers will contrast, 'cause luck like this will forever last. The fellows are all green with envy wondering why it had to be me that's so lucky.

I'm so lucky it's clear to see; you release the endorphins in me. No superstition or witchcraft. Just repetitive pleasure is what I have. I get so excited it makes my laugh.

I'm so lucky, I'm so lucky!

❦

Won't Be No Fool

I had water in my eyes the day she walked right out my life. I thought my world had come to an end, because she was my first girlfriend.

But time can heal all things, and now here she comes again. Now I have experience as my friend, that she'd break your heart in the end.

Break your heart is what she'll do.

Break your heart is what she'll do.

So I told her that breaking hearts is what you do, and I won't be no fool for you.

Breaking hearts is what you do, and I won't be no fool for you.

Playing games is your claim to fame, breaking hearts and causing pain.

You know my love won't be the same, because I know how to play your game.

Now, isn't it a shame that someone has turned your sunshine into rain?

So I told her that breaking hearts is what you do, and I won't be no fool for you.

Breaking hearts is what you do, and I won't be no fool for you. Playing games is your claim to fame, breaking hearts and causing pain.

I won't be no fool for you, 'cause I know how to break hearts, too.

Love Crimes

It ought to be a crime the way you spend your time, thinking that a good man is hard to find.

If only you knew what to do with a love that's so true, you wouldn't think that I was just another one of your fools.

You thought that you had a fool, but you had no clue that I really loved you.

But now you've let this good man slip through your hands like grains of sand.

So, now you can play your games running around town, loving your men, and then putting them down.

I was that good man that slipped through your hands like grains of sand.

My love was so true, but you played me for your fool.

All your false love signs should be a crime.

It was an offense, on the time that I spent.

It was an assault, on the passion that couldn't be bought.

It was a violation, to end our relations.

The love crime you'll commit is to love a good man and then split.

So, now you can play your game all around town, loving them and putting them down.

You like to spend your time committing love crimes.

So Wrong

How could something so wrong be so right?

When we met that warm summer night.

We both had significant others in our life, your husband and my wife.

How can something feel so wrong, seem so right for only one night? We both could see that this feeling should never be.

As we talked, I can see you can feel my small crush; that made you blush. Before we let that feeling grow strong, we needed to act responsible because we both had loved ones at home.

The Devil on my left told me to hold her, the Angel on the right said to take flight. Loving you would be so wrong, it couldn't be right, and it's a sin in God's sight.

So, I had to say goodbye. And pray and say to God; forgive me for thinking in that way.

Dreams of Romance

When you came into my dream, you took my breath away. I tossed, turned and yearned for your touch. Oh how I wanted you so much.

Your brown eyes had me hypnotized. As if I was paralyzed, I was so emotionally incapacitated.

Nevertheless, I didn't hesitate to seal my fate.

My destiny has gotten the best of me. It's inevitably that you return to me nightly in my dreams.

My dreams of romance, ooh dreams of romance, oh my dreams.

When you come to me, you set my sprit free.

I anticipate the romance you give me.

My dreams of romance, ooh dreams of romance, oh my dreams.

When I awake, you seemed so real, I spend my days looking for your feel.

My dreams of romance, ooh dreams of romance, oh my dreams.

This feeling's got to be real.

My dreams of romance, ooh dreams of romance, oh my dreams.

Ooh my dreams.

Love Disorder

I fell in love and now I can't get up, I sit in my lonely room in gloom; my girl has left me so blue, the pain feels like the flu.

I've loved her into my bad health, I got nausea, I got chills and I went to see the doctor all he had was a pill.

I need my baby to take away this fever her love can cure, without her love I'll have to endure.

In the school of love I should've been smarter, but now she left me with a love disorder.

I'm suffering from love lost as a terminal condition, someone has stole my love and it sent me into a funk.

I have heartaches and pain losing my baby's love has driven me insane, someone took her like a theft in the night. She gone and I couldn't even put up a fight.

I had no premonition that my baby would ever come up missing her love kept me strong, now I'm feeling sick and wondering where did I go wrong.

I wish I had an intuition to be smarter, but now I sit here with a love disorder.

⚘

Damaged

When I met her, I tried to lay down my cards, so I spoke from my heart, but her anger was provoked and I could tell that her heart's been broke.

She's been hurt so bad before, the pain emanating from her couldn't be ignored.

I could see that she can be a sweetie, but the men in her past has treated her so shitty. Brothers I know from the 'hood would say that she's damage goods.

Someone has left her with such heavy baggage; it's running her ragged.

Her compass to love had her going in circles.

She feels true love is a myth and it doesn't exist, because she's been through too much love shit.

A fellow once told her that the reason he lies is that he doesn't like to see her cry.

Her last man told her that the reason why he hit and bruised her is that he doesn't want to lose her.

Her resistance intensified my persistence.

I thought I had the love and care she needed so desperately for repair.

But, she had no trust to invest and the pain has her drained.

She feels all the love she depleted has her defeated; with her love someone took advantage and now she's damaged.

❦

Love Land

While on the road to Love, I've gone into the town of Trouble, and if you've ever been through Trouble on your way to Love then you know that's no place you want to stay for long.

I had to move on and quick, then I found myself in Fear.

I was in Fear thinking that I would never end up in Love, and Fear wasn't too far from Trouble. But I stayed in Fear for about four days. I moved around so much until I was at the edge of Fear and that's when I met a pretty young lady that lead me into Fantasy Land.

I knew I was in Fantasy Land because everything I fantasized about doing with her came true. One night, she asked me if I'd ever been in Love and I said no, but that's where I'm headed. She asked me how long did I plan to stay there. I said as long as I can. Hopefully, 'til I die.

I asked her, if she's ever been in Love and she said yes many times before. I asked her what was it like being in Love?

She said it could be nice and warm. The sun can shine every day with no clouds; it can make you feel so happy you'll want to stay there forever. But it can be cold and dark as well, and it can hurt like hell, until your heart can't take it anymore.

She said in order to stay in Love and ease the pain, you will sometimes walk around headed to a State of Make Believe. I asked where is that State?

She replied that "The State of Make Believe" is while you're in Love, you will have to make it and believe it into what you want it to be. Then the hurt will most likely subside.

She also told me that if you don't do your part while in Love, you can end up living in Fear, in Trouble or just in Lonely Town, and I've been there before and I couldn't live like that.

So, I asked her if she would take me to Love Land and show me how to live. She told me to lead the way, and now that I am living in Love I'll take her over to Paradise every night for a little fun.

Help Thy Neighbor

Well, I just love making my way throughout my day on my porch. I see my neighbors come and go off to work to make their pay; I just wave and nod, because I have nothing to say.

I've sat and watched the neighborhood bully take the kids' candy. I see him all the time; I think his name is Randy.

He looked me right in the eyes the other day, but I just turned away, because I have nothing to say.

Minding my own business, on my porch, is all I want to do. I once witnessed Mr. Turner beat his wife 'til she was black and blue. I think he was trying to make her stay. I just shook my head, because I have nothing to say.

My porch has become my sanctuary; I just sit here and think all day, because I have nothing to say.

When I pick up the morning paper to start my day, I read it from page to page and the current events say that things are looking gray. I just place it face down, because I have nothing to say.

The postman passed my way today. He handed me a letter from the bank that stated in bolded letters, FORECLOSURE.

Now my mortgage, I know, I must pay; but with the increase in rates, the bank won't give me the time of day, because I do have something to say!

I Can't Trust My Uncle

Peek-a-boo I see you and the things that you do.

Peek-a-boo I see you and the people do, too.

My uncle is like, making a promise, but with your fingers crossed.

My uncle is like, a dope fiend pacing the floor at the Betty Ford.

My uncle is like, catching your mate on a cheating date.

As a resident, I try to remain humble. But I must confess, I can't trust my uncle. You catch him in a lie, he starts to buckle. I must confess, I can't trust my uncle.

Peek-a-boo I see you and the wrong things that you do.

Peek-a-boo I see you and God does, too.

My uncle continues to test my cognition. From the shores
of Africa through the waters of Katrina; the Tuskegee experiment
into the search for weapons of mass destruction.

 In this land with good and plenty of ill-gotten gains, my uncle's
name is Sam and I don't think he gives a damn who I am.

Peek-a-boo I see you and some of the good things that you do.
Like sending the troops to rebuild after you send them to kill.

Peek-a –boo I see you.

My cognitive ability allows me to see my dubious uncle's trickery.
So I will say, peek –a-boo, I see you and soon the family will, too!

꽃

Trials and Tribulations or Peace and Tranquility

It was once asked, "What good is it for a man to gain the whole world, yet forfeit his soul?"

Peace & Tranquility—Trials & Tribulations
Our love and pride of this country/our despair because of non-acceptance

Peace & Tranquility—Trials & Tribulations
We love seeing our black president in office and on television/be we hate the way he is being treated.

Peace & Tranquility—Trials & Tribulations
Our language toward one another, i.e., What's up my Nigga?/ I'll kill you Nigga!
Peace & Tranquility—Trials & Tribulations

Our sisters' endless love for their brothers and our brothers' for their sisters/but our negative stereotypes and conflicts we often cast upon one other, i.e., she's a stuck-up bitch or he's a dog/no job.

Peace & Tranquility—Trials &Tribulations
Our brotherly love the million-man march showed us/our gangbanging activity throughout the decades proves self-hate.

Peace &Tranquility
Once we respect ourselves and accept our black skin, big lips and kinky hair.

Trials & Tribulations
Disrespecting ourselves in and out of public and changing our features to appease other folks, to make them comfortable.

Ever since that day Marvin Gaye went away, I'm still wondering, what's going on?

But with God's will I know our peace & tranquility, as a people, will come to fruition.

And our Trials & Tribulations will become only trials to be won!!

Justice

Oh say, did you hear? It was by dawn's early light that bitch America had a bastard child. She was so proud she named her Justice; and we would love to hold her up to the twilight.

America said that Justice was for all of us; but Justice couldn't see us all. You see, Justice is blind; America's foundation caused Justice birth defective. So, I say

America, America how can Justice be for me?

Due to the fact America was a whore at the time. She couldn't remember who she fucked or whom she fucked over. With her past, it could've been incest.

So Justice is blind and sometimes unbalanced. However, Justice promises to prevail. Some of us embraced Justice, and some of us never will receive Justice. So, I say

America, America how can Justice be for me?

The world has admired and feared America, with her misappropriation of power. Unlike America, always working for a new and cheap thrill, Justice vowed to work for humanity.

So, I say to America, Yes Justice is for me!!

Sick Mind,
Body and Soul

Lady America is sick Mind, Body and Soul. And she is refusing help to heal. For example, a powerful philosopher with a surname of X tried to heal the <u>mind</u> of America by holding a mirror up to her face, but she feared what she saw and assassinated him.

Camelot sent a duo team of brothers: John and Bobby. They tried to work in the body of America by fixing the nucleus-functions that maintain the integrity of the <u>body</u>, but due to her early bad behaviors, the cancer has sat in. So, she's decaying inside and now all she can think about is building jail cells while her main organs are hurting like hell. So, America felt that these brothers were doing more harm than good. So, she assassinated them both.

A Dr. King once paid a visit, and the world knew that he had the antidote for saving the <u>soul</u> of America, but she didn't like the taste. America said that she felt too well balanced. You see, a medicine that works for the good sometimes leaves a bad taste, and morally America can't live with that. So, she assassinated him.

America would rather pacify herself by spending her sick days with yearly sporting events and seasonal holidays of make believe, i.e. Santa Claus, Easter Bunny, Ghosts/Goblins and etc. She loves watching reality shows and ignoring her own reality, which is facing her ills with racism, fixing the unjust ways she treats the core of her body, and accepting the change that is needed to make her healthier and grow with strength to become a better America. "Mind Body And Soul"

My Philosophy on the Cheating Man

Now, I do not believe that all men cheat, especially as often as their options.

I don't know many men who would prefer fast food out in the street rather than the good cooked food they have at home.

I don't know many men who would rather have a relationship with two or more women; opposed to one good woman. And if she were a good woman why would you cheat? Normally a man wouldn't cross his male friend that he has had a good friendship with, it just wouldn't make sense.

On the other hand, research has shown that men have a higher desire for sex than women. At the start of the relationship, usually the sexual attraction is one of the main things that keep the relationship going, and the sex is really an ongoing thing.

It may come to a point and time where the man can really get accustomed to that level of sexual activity that he is receiving in the relationship.

At the same time, it may come to a point where the woman can't continue at the level of sexual activity in which the relationship started. Although, she will still enjoy being with the man, an emotional issue or just her lack of desire can put an end to that level of activity.

The man, on the other hand, has a higher desire or craving than his counter part so he is living with the expectations of having some kind of sexual intercourse, almost to the level of that in which he once knew at the start of the relationship.

It is something like having a midnight craving some will get while up at night, but can't get to the snacks. Or it can seem as if working on a job and your boss asked you to take a pay cut, because the economy is slow. And now, he knows that his pay will never be where it once was.

So, in order to fulfill his sexual desires or to get his pay back to where it once was, he takes on another woman at the same time he's in the current relationship. He may take on a second job while he's working the first job. Some men will take on this behavior at any cost, something like a junkie.

The woman can sometimes disregard the man's desire or cravings, as if she feels things are just fine with the level of intercourse. Subsequently, some men will eventually throw their integrity and morals out the window to fulfill that desire.

Now this behavior can be acceptable or okay with some women, but it's cheating when the woman does not approve or isn't aware.

For the man to have integrity means doing the right thing when no one is watching. If not, it can be a bad case of immaturity.

For the man to have morals in the relationship means conforming to standards of what is right or just behavior.

Keep in mind, integrity and morals are a necessity, in which some men will need to help refrain from cheating.

❦

www.ingramcontent.com/pod-product-compliance
Lightning Source LLC
Chambersburg PA
CBHW021913040426
42447CB00007B/844